Saving the World.....
.....One Latte at a Time

The Story of
Homer's Coffee House

By

Jim Mathis

Edited by
Bob Tamasy
And
John Indellicate II

Jun 20, 2006

Barbara
I hope you enjoy
this & future visits
to Homers.
Love in Christ
Tony Maden
tonymaden@
yahoo.com

Published by:
Kansas City CBMC, Inc
7126 W 80th St
Overland Park, KS 66204

Cover design and photos by Jim Mathis

www.HomersCoffeeHouse.com

jimmydmathis@hotmail.com

ISBN: 0-9773055-0-3

Special thanks to Steve Denyes for the use of the phrase:
"Saving the World...One Latte at a Time"
from his song:

One Latte at a Time
Copyright by Steve Denyes
www.SteveDenyes.com

Susan Ford's a double latte, easy on the foam
Robert Clark's a house large, with a blueberry scone.
You can go ahead a quiz me, but I can tell you from the start. I know every name and every order by heart.

This is not rocket science, I'm not curing cancer,
I'm not the one they come to when they're looking for answers.
But I think you'll find I'm a hero of a kind,
Just saving the world, one latte at a time.

I make the mornings of the movers and shakers,
I tell jokes to the coffee breakers,
I serve high tea to the PTA,
They all come to see me to start their day.

I make a living turning water and beans,
Into this towns daily dose of caffeine.

This is not rocket science, I'm not curing cancer,
I'm not the one they come to when they're looking for answers.
But I think you'll find I'm a hero of a kind,
Just saving the world, one latte at a time.

Table of Contents

Foreword - 6

Introduction - 8

The Scene - 9

New Year's Eve Challenge -10

How do you get there from here? -12

Leaving Engineering, Heading to the Bars -16

Photography and the World of Proper Etiquette - 23

Seeing the World in Black and White - 25

Going Into Business for Ourselves - 27

The Experience of a Lifetime - 30

Children: To Have, or Not to Have? - 33

The Spiritual Side of Parenting - 35

How to Best Invest Our Time and Careers? - 37

My Father, the Auctioneer - 42

Determined Not to Have Any Regrets - 44

Addressing the Uniqueness of New Generations - 46

Finally Answering the Challenge - 47

Homer Anderson: A Worthy Namesake - 51

Solving Finances By Recognizing Interests - 53

Homer's: The Dream Comes True – 56

I Corinthians 13 Paraphrase - 58

It's About The Music - 60

A Unique, Eclectic Community - 65

Foreword

The first time I met Homer Anderson was in 1981, and I had the privilege of spending time with him and his wife, Wilma, on several occasions after that. It was amazing how such a humble, unassuming individual could possess such a passion for communicating the Good News of Jesus Christ to as many people as possible.

Working quietly but faithfully behind the scenes, Homer first championed servicemen's centers during and after World War II, and then Mayor's Prayer Breakfasts throughout Kansas, convinced that men and women needed to hear about the peace, hope and meaning in life that could only be found in Jesus. Even while wrestling with the ravages of Parkinson's Disease, Homer never lost sight of his mission – or his zeal.

I did not meet Jim and Louise Mathis until years later, but almost immediately we became fast friends, partly because of our mutual interest in photography, as well as our commitment to serving God and others. However, I have not had an opportunity to visit the Kansas City area since Homer's Coffee House was established, so this engaging little book has been a special treat, allowing me to learn about its what's and how's and why's.

Saving the World...One Latte at a Time gives a unique perspective on how the reality of Jesus Christ and the practicality of His truths can be incarnated over a cup of coffee (with or without caffeine). The notion of linking Jesus and java is not some whimsical idea, but an innovative approach for combining our fascination with a fresh-brewed cup and our innate need for community and place. Years ago we saw this depicted by the neighborhood bar in the TV sitcom, *Cheers*. Homer's Coffee House is proving that camaraderie and compassion can be as compelling an attraction as alcohol.

Homer Anderson never lived to visit the coffee house named for him, but I feel certain he would have approved, giving it his ringing endorsement. Anything to introduce people to Jesus, whether it takes place in a large, cavernous banquet hall or the quaint, intimate confines of a coffee house. I suspect that if Jesus were to return today, He would opt for the coffee house.

So enjoy your literary tour of Homer's Coffee House. You will find that, like the bar in *Cheers,* it's a place where everybody knows your name – and they're always glad you came.

Robert J. Tamasy
Chattanooga, Tennessee

Introduction

Since Homer's Coffee House opened in 2001, a lot of people have asked questions like how Homer's came to exist, who Homer was, or why we do things the way we do. The purpose of this book is to answer some of these questions. It is also intended to share a little bit of the vision and mission that is embodied in the coffeehouse.

I hope to communicate some ideas about spiritual gifts, skill, talent, and passion. I believe I was called by God to operate a Christian coffeehouse. That does not mean that I heard a voice in a thunderstorm or a stone tablet was handed down from heaven with instructions written on it. It only means that I was given a specific set of gifts, skills, and passions, and that I have had unique experiences that cause me to believe that this is what I need to be doing with my life at this time. I believe that each experience in life prepares us for the next. Perhaps you will be able to see more clearly from my experiences how Homer's Coffee House came to be.

We hope that this book will encourage our supporters, patrons, artists, performers, and staff. We also hope that it will be a benefit to others who wish to follow our path, seeking to become a light in their community.

Mission Blues at Homer's

The Scene

"Homer's is a wonderful place. There is so much great fellowship. There are young people and old people, married people and single people, people with kids and people without kids, Christians and non-Christians, and the sense of community is beyond any one of us. Homer's is the most amazing place I've ever been in my life."

Penny Fairman, Stay-at-home mom and poet.

Penny's view is far from unique. At any time of day, there are several groups of people meeting at Homer's Coffee House. Some are there for Bible studies, some for a CPR class or a writer's group, or others just hanging out with friends. The mornings before work and evenings after work are busiest, of course, but throughout the day people drift in out for a coffee break, to meet a friend, or just to see what is going on in the neighborhood.

On Friday and Saturday nights the mood is transformed as musical groups of all kinds take to the stage for two hours of family entertainment. Homer's features singer/songwriter's, jazz, and country; but Christian rock and blues are always near by. Homer's is now known as Kansas City's home of Christian blues, and the place to be if you are a Christian musician in the Midwest.

But how did this happen? What was the vision behind the place?

New Year's Eve Challenge

December 31, 1999 – The world was anxiously waiting for the new millennium. Would the Y2K bug strike and disable many of the world's computers? Who knew? But I wasn't all that concerned. My concern was that four years earlier I had sold a successful business to follow God's call to vocational ministry and, so far, my main accomplishment had been spending the proceeds of the sale and part of my life's savings.

My staff position with CBMC USA (Christian Businessmen's Committee USA) called for me to minister to the needs of business and professional men in the Kansas City area, and my task was to determine how best to accomplish that mission.

One of our CBMC leaders, Gary Tenpenny, had offered to buy me lunch and give the ministry an old laptop computer. Over lunch Gary asked an important question: "What are you going to do to make a difference in the next few years, the new millennium?" Any year that ends in three zeros seems to take on extra significance, so with the year 2000 looming, it was a timely question.

That challenge ultimately led to the opening, twenty-one months later, of Homer's Coffee House in downtown Overland Park, Kansas, an upscale suburb of Kansas City and our home for the past 34 years. Homer's motto is "Saving the world…one latte at a time."

Getting to the place in life where I thought that selling coffee was going to change the world is not that easy to explain. For me to do that, it might help to give you a little bit about my background. Without question, personal experiences have played a significant role in the development of Homer's Coffee House. Each of us has unique experiences which God uses to prepare us for the next challenge or calling, and that has definitely been true for me in seeing Homer's move from an idea to reality.

How do you get there from here?

I was a privileged child. By that I mean that I had a mother and father who loved each other and loved me. That puts me in the minority as I understand it. I also grew up in Southeast Kansas, a part of the country that had never really recovered from the Great Depression. Even though it was the prosperous '50s in some places, nobody I knew had money for nice houses, new cars, or more than one pair of shoes. I can't remember a single person in my hometown of Dearing, Kansas that ever bought a car new. That's also part of the privileged part. There was little sense of entitlement. Working hard just to get by was considered normal. Expectations weren't all that high.

Music has been my passion for as long as I can remember. My earliest memory is of going to a concert and crying because I wanted to be on stage playing music. I couldn't understand why I couldn't just get up and play. I was probably three years old. My dad, Vern Mathis, played guitar and sang, as did my mom, Joan. Actually my dad was not just a musician – he was a performer. He was a pretty good singer and played guitar enough to get by, but he seemed to come alive in front of a group of people. I didn't realize until years later what a special gift that was. I don't think he thought about it as gift because he didn't see why other people weren't the same way. I now know that God gives each of us gifts and we are all different. He was able to use this gift to good advantage, not as an entertainer, but as an auctioneer. For most of my childhood we had a family business, Mathis Auction Co. Mathis Auction operated a weekly consignment sale on

Monday nights as well as estate and farm sales. My dad also conducted an auction in Tulsa, Oklahoma every Tuesday night. Growing up around auctions was a good education. Supply and demand is not a foreign concept to me at all. If nobody wants something, it has no value. If a lot of people want it, the value is high. That's the way auctions work.

My dad also had a band for a while. In actuality, it was just a group of guys who got together to do what they enjoyed, and occasionally, people would come to hear them. One of the guys was a steel guitar player named Lee Pettijohn. Lee played a triple neck Fender through a big Fender tweed amp. Lee also repaired televisions for a living. Lee became my hero, so I learned to play the steel guitar and repair TVs.

My mother, Virginia Joan Olson Mathis Timmerman, is the granddaughter of Swedish immigrants. She grew up in the farming community of Labette County, Kansas. She worked for Southwestern Bell, first as an operator and then in management. She retired from SBC with about forty years seniority. I usually think of her as the only person in the family to ever have a steady job. "Solid" is a good way to describe her. She plays the guitar and has a pretty singing voice. She started her musical career when she was about eight, performing in a talent show in Mound Valley, Kansas.

In the fifth grade I joined the Dearing Bees 4-H Club (Head, Heart, Hands, & Health). In 4-H, I studied electricity and photography, but also raised chickens. I bought one hundred chicks every spring. We slaughtered the males for frying, but kept the hens for laying. Before long I had built up a pretty good flock of laying hens. I sold eggs door to door from my first car, a 1952 Pontiac.

I got involved judging chickens and entered poultry judging contests locally and at the Kansas State Fair in Hutchinson. I spent many days and nights at the State Fair. To this day, If I go to the Missouri State Fair in Sedalia, I head straight for the poultry barns; the chickens are like old friends.

We have had a long-standing joke in our family that I am going to get some chickens and get back in the egg business. However, my wife, Louise, always reminds me that Overland Park isn't zoned for chickens and that ends the discussion. Recently I was talking to an Overland Park city councilman when he mentioned "the chicken deal." I asked him what he meant, and he told me that they had just issued a special use permit for some kids to raise chickens near downtown Overland Park. (They were 4-H members, too) Who knew? Perhaps I could have had chickens all this time!

My family also had Shetland ponies, Duroc & Hampshire hogs, and Angora goats. I saved my egg money to buy a tape recorder – a Webcor. I had bought a new high-end Akai tape recorder by the time I left for college. I recorded bands and other musical groups. In high school, I designed, and had built, a recording console for use by the music department.

My friends and I also experimented with car audio. I had a 45 rpm turntable mounted in the glove compartment with speakers in the back and under the seats. This was before eight-tracks or cassettes and twenty years before CDs were invented. When I hear kids driving down the street with twenty speakers and 1,000 watt plus car stereos, I remember what we used to try to do before any of the current high-powered stuff was available. (As I write this, I realize this seems like verbal carbon-dating - I seem to be showing my age.)

In high school, I played in the band and took vocational electronics classes. I was an "A" student, on the Honor Roll, and a member of the National Honor Society. "Geek" was a bad word in those days. I tried to avoid it. I attended Labette County Community High School in Altamont, Kansas. LCCHS was a consolidated school and drew from a large geographical area. I drove thirty-five miles from Dearing each way every day. Altamont was very strong in the performing arts for a rural high school. I was involved in orchestra, band, and school musicals. I enrolled in beginner band and when the band director asked what instrument I played, I said whatever was needed. By my sophomore year I was the first chair tuba player. Playing tuba got me interested in Dixieland music, the beginning of a very eclectic music background that I would acquire.

A big problem in small towns is "brain drain" and I, like a lot of other kids in town, couldn't wait to get out. Most of us never went back. I went to Kansas State University in Manhattan, Kansas, mainly because it was the proper distance from Dearing. Two hundred miles was far enough to start a new life, but close enough to get home on one tank of gas if need be.

Sure enough, K-State was a whole new world. Freshman orientation started with a party and a live band. I was mesmerized.

Leaving Engineering, Heading to the Bars

My college plans were to forget about music and become an electrical engineer. But the college music scene of the sixties quickly distracted me. I had spent the summers repairing televisions and doing real world electronics stuff, so vector theory and the other things they were teaching in engineering school seemed totally boring and unimportant. I also soon learned that I was not the same type of person as the other engineering students. Art and music majors were more "my people." I wrote a thesis on the history of stereophonic sound and quietly left engineering school.

The bands at the local clubs were much more exciting. I decided I could play electric bass, bought a used Fender Jazz Bass and a Fender Showman amp, and started telling all the bands that came through that I was a bass player. Obviously, my experience as a bass player was pretty limited.

I am the oldest of three boys. My brother, Chester, was born the day I started to school in the first grade. My other brother, Joe, was born ten years later, when I was in high school. Chester was always the most musical in the family and is currently very involved in music ministry. Joe gravitated more toward Broadway musicals. One is more likely to catch him in a community theater stage production than playing in a band. Chester and I, on the other hand, decided that we wanted to be instrumentalists. We had a family band: My mother, dad, Chester and I performed at community events around Montgomery County. I played the steel guitar and it was decided that Chester should play bass. My dad hired an old family friend, Rodney Lay, to give both Chester and me some bass lessons.

Rodney had considerable success playing rock and roll in the early sixties. Those were the days of pompadour haircuts and gold lamé suits. I remember Rodney saying that he had made hundreds of thousands of dollars in 1961, '62, & '63, but he had blown it all. He said he regretted his lifestyle and financial choices, and wished he had all that money back. That thought has always stayed with me. Just because one is making money now, it may not be here next year. Rodney kept his 1962 Cadillac for years as a reminder.

Rodney and his band, Rodney and the Blazers, later became Roy Clark's road band. When Roy became the co-host of the syndicated television show, "Hee-Haw," Rodney became its musical director. Rodney later bought the "Roy Clark Theater" in Branson, Missouri and was the first person to bring national artists to that little Missouri town. Like my family, Rodney frequently had gone to Branson on family weekends and saw its potential.

Music had never been easy for me. I grew up with the idea that talent meant that you could do something without working at it. By that definition, I was not talented. I spent many hours practicing the steel guitar, beginning when I was eight years old and no one ever called me a child prodigy. I took up the bass because I thought it would be easier and every band had a bass player.

It was the fall of 1966 when I got a call from Mark Allerheiligen, the leader of a bar band that needed a bass player. He had been playing the bass lines on the organ for a few weeks and figured anybody loud would do. Mark and I played together for the next five years. Our band had a number of musical variations, playing everything from blues to British invasion covers.

We never considered ourselves to be great artists, but we did make a lot of money. In those days before disco, 1966 to 1971, bands could work as much as they wanted if they didn't mind fraternity parties and redneck bars. We played about three nights a week and made more money than our buddies who were working construction five days a week. I never quite figured out how club owners could sell 25 cent draws and dollar pitchers of beer and still pay the band $200, but that was their business.

We played a steady circuit of bars and roadhouses throughout Kansas and Nebraska. We also played in Arkansas, Oklahoma, New Mexico, and Colorado. Some of the places got a little rowdy. You know, the types of places where they check you for guns at the door - and if you don't have one, they give you one. I have actually played places where chicken wire was used to protect the band from flying chairs and beer bottles. (It works, too.) Occasional high school proms or college parties were nice diversions. We even spent some time in a recording studio, but nothing ever came of it. Regardless, it was good experience.

We had several names over the five years, "Blue Valley Sand & Gravel Company," "The Playmates," and "Autum." The main thing we did was drive. It was not uncommon to have two "gigs" five hundred miles apart. At one point we were driving about 100,000 miles a year. Those were the days of twenty-five cent gas, but tires seldom lasted 12,000 miles. Looking back, it was really just one long road trip, stopping occasionally to play music. A few years later when Willie Nelson sang, "On the road again, life I love is making music with my friends, I can't wait to get on the road again," I knew exactly what he was talking about.

Sometimes traveling itself was an adventure. On one occasion, we left Manhattan in the morning heading for a Saturday night dance in Guyman, Oklahoma. Somewhere east of Dodge City it began to rain, quickly turning to ice. Before long we were doing about twenty miles an hour with a half of inch of ice on the road and the van. About that time the throttle linkage broke. On a '67 Ford Econoline, the engine sits between the driver and passenger and the front is not well-protected. We managed to limp into the Ford dealer in Dodge. When we found out that a part would have to be sent out from Wichita, we called the club to tell them we couldn't make it. They had been trying to get in touch with us to tell they were canceling because of the storm. We rigged up a temporary linkage with a wire to run the throttle by hand. We turned around and headed home, arriving back in Manhattan about twenty hours after we left, having driven almost the entire time on ice.

I had three jobs in the band. In addition to playing bass, I kept all the electronic equipment in good repair, and did all the driving. I'm not sure how I ended up being the driver, but I was certainly more comfortable behind the wheel than riding with other musicians in questionable states of consciousness and sobriety.

Jim Mathis with Gibson EB-O in Hugoton, Kansas - 1968

Like most bands of the era, we had a hard time hearing ourselves. We tried lots of different positions for the PA speakers, but nothing worked very well. We eventually decided to buy a whole additional PA system and split the sound to the two systems with one set of speakers pointing back at us. This is, of course, standard practice today with all sorts of stage monitor set-ups. I am sure that we were not the first band to use stage monitors, but we were among the first, and we had to figure out how to do it ourselves.

I started out playing the Fender Jazz Bass but soon discovered the Gibson EB-O. The Gibson had a shorter neck and a faster action, so it was easier to play. It also produced the low-end "thud" we were looking for. My first EB-O was stolen from the Experimental Light Farm in Manhattan. I quickly bought another identical guitar. I traded that one for a Gibson Les Paul Bass in 1970. The Les Paul had the fast Gibson neck, but with two pick-ups and enough switches to produce about any sound one would want. I still have the Les Paul and play it frequently.

As for amplifiers, I switched from the regular Showman to a Dual Showman, and then added an extra cabinet. Eventually I was playing through a Kustom amp with six 15 inch JBL speakers. Needless to say, it was loud. I am paying for that now with a substantial hearing loss. My father, grandmother and grandfather were all hard of hearing, so I am sure that is a big factor as well.

The only time that seemed short was the time actually playing. Fortunately, most gigs were at least three hours. I am always surprised when bands play an hour and think they have played a long show. Even though I never considered myself a great musician, playing on the bandstand nine hours plus per week, week after week, I became very confident of my ability.

This was a time of great social change and we were right in the middle of it. In 1966 and 1967 we had short hair and wore suits and ties to class. (Remember the Beach Boys, the Temptations, and the Beatles?) By

1968 everyone had hair down to their waist, and tie-dies and sandals were the fashion. (Think Grateful Dead, Jefferson Airplane) I wanted to play in a band because of Elvis - with fancy suits and Cadillacs. By the time I got there, it was cut-off jeans, T-shirts, and VW buses.

At one point around 1967, Vernon Cluke became our drummer. Cluke was a short, stocky black guy. Since he lived close to me, I usually picked him up to ride to the gigs. I didn't think much about it, but I soon became aware that we came from very different cultures. He exposed me to soul food and Wolfman Jack, and I exposed him to Bob Wills and Western Swing. He wasn't surprised, but I was, when restaurants refused to serve us. We would rather drive all night than be humiliated by hotels that wouldn't accept blacks. I didn't become a civil rights activist after that, but I certainly came face to face with the problem and developed an understanding of the reality and the pain caused by prejudice.

I was still trying to go to college, and by my junior year had changed my major to business with an emphasis on finance. Music would have been a more logical choice, but the classical music education taught in college at that time did not appeal to me.

In the fifties and sixties at least, if it is not still the case, formal music training consisted of teaching people to play notes. I guess the idea is if you play notes one after the other, it will sound a little bit like music. Most non-musicians know that music is about feel, mood, emotion, and connecting with the heart. The music majors I knew had already forgotten that. For that reason I never seriously considered music school, even though music was clearly my passion.

Finance was a good choice for my college major because it gave me a very good background for business. I always knew that I would have my own business. Even as a young person, working for a corporation had no appeal. Learning about economics, accounting, banking, and financial management provided a good basis for operating a small business.

Photography and the World of Proper Etiquette

My other passion was photography. As a child I wanted to express myself visually, but a second grade teacher laughed at my art and told me I couldn't draw. Of course, I believed her. Since painting starts with drawing, becoming a painter was out of the question. In the fourth grade I got my first camera. Realizing that I could express myself without drawing turned on a light and, besides, my photographs were just as good as those made by the adults I knew.

In college, I started hanging out with other photographers and thanks to playing music, was able to make enough money to buy a 35mm single-lens-reflex camera and a few lenses. I started going to art galleries and reading every photo book I could find. Before long I had enough skill that I could photograph anything I could see. All I needed to do was learn how to see. This has turned out to be a lifelong learning experience.

By this time I was spending all my time playing music, making photographs, or drinking coffee with my friends. This was a great education, but it didn't lead to a degree. My college career ended with a fizzle and I didn't return for what would have been my fifth year. I considered my time at Kansas State a first-class four-year education, though I learned more outside the classroom than in. That, however, was not what the university thought added up to a degree, so I left K-State without a diploma.

At Kansas State, I was a member of Alpha Kappa Lambda fraternity. AKL in those days was into civilized living – big time. My freshman year was pretty much a boot camp for good manners. Any AKL in those days could have written a book on manners and etiquette. As pledges we could be, and were, demerited or fined for such infractions as picking up the wrong fork, taking a drink of water without wiping our mouth with a napkin, or failing to open a door for a lady. After a while all those things became second nature. I have never forgotten them and consequently have never been uncomfortable going to fancy restaurants or other formal social settings. I have, however, stopped noticing other people's faux pas as much, and I no longer consider passing the bread with the wrong hand a criminal offense.

At a fraternity party my freshman year, I meant an amazing, beautiful girl. She was the most elegant, graceful person I had ever seen. For the next four years I kept track of her, but seldom spoke to her and never asked her out. I guess I was intimidated by the fact that at 6 foot 2 inches, Louise Wall was at least two inches taller than I and the tallest woman I knew. I eventually arranged for us to be at the same dinner party. After dating several months, we married on September 4, 1971. I could not ask for a better partner in marriage, business, and life. She is and always will be the love of my life - and it only took me four years to ask her out!

By the time Louise and I were ready to get married, playing in clubs and driving thousands of miles had lost its appeal. I told Mark and the other guys to go on without me and I got a job selling cameras at Ben's Camera Exchange, 205 E 12th Street, Kansas City, Missouri in May, 1971. Louise and I were married in September, and she moved to Kansas City in January 1972 after she graduated from Kansas State. Needless to say, that was a stressful year, planning a wedding, getting married, and then not living together for four months.

Louise had studied in France between high school and college, majored in French and was planning to teach. A bad student-teaching experience, however, convinced her to do something else. Before long, she was an insurance underwriter with CNA Insurance. When the CNA Regional Office closed, she began working for Pyramid Life Insurance.

Seeing the World in Black and White

Ben's Camera dealt in professional level cameras and accessories, so I soon became familiar with the photographers, studios, labs, and galleries in Kansas City. The conventional wisdom was that black and white was on the way out and color was the wave of the future. Several black and white photos labs closed while I was at Ben's. When the lab that was doing Ben's black and white processing closed, I volunteered to do the work myself at home. I loved black and white and had spent many hours studying the classical black and white photographers - Ansel Adams, Edward Weston, and Alfred Stieglitz..

I quickly began making as much money at home in the darkroom as I was during the day selling cameras. I began to add outside commercial clients such as Bethany Medical Center. In June 1974, I left Ben's to work full-time in the darkroom. A year later, Louise left Pyramid Life and joined me in the photo business.

Going Into Business for Ourselves

Jim and Louise at Mathis Photo - 1994

For fifteen years we worked at home in our basement darkroom. We intentionally decided to keep our business small and just did the work we could do ourselves. Of course, black and white photography did not die, and in fact, went through a bit of a renaissance in the seventies and eighties that continues to this day. We developed a reputation as the black and white experts in town. Our business consisted of processing black and white film, making prints, and restoring and copying vintage photographs. For years we were the only place in Kansas City that could print from antique negatives or glass plates. The Johnson County Historical Museum was one of our bigger customers.

In 1983 we decided that we didn't need more money, but rather more time. We decided to only work Monday through Thursday and always be closed on Friday, Saturday, and Sunday. We kept this schedule for thirteen years, from 1983 to 1996.

In 1988 we moved to a store front at 7801 Floyd in Overland Park. We opened a beautiful photo lab and studio. Black and white portraits became a big part of our business. Actors, musicians, and other performers were a big part of our portrait business as were realtors, business people, and politicians. To some people's view, we were obsessed with quality. We insisted on only the highest quality work from ourselves. We never tried to compete on price, but aimed for the quality end of the market. This quality approach to business and a commitment to customer service meant that we always had plenty of work.

The Floyd Avenue address also gave me a place to display my antique camera collection. I had become interested in old cameras when I was working at Ben's. Kenny Young, the owner of Ben's Camera, was a collector and I would occasionally go to camera shows with him. I began studying the history of photography and buying cameras and accessories that I thought were historically significant. I even had an 1888 Kodak, the first camera to carry that name. It was the camera that brought photography to the masses and launched the photofinishing industry. Before The Kodak, photography was a complicated affair practiced only by professionals or serious hobbyists.

I set up a photography museum in the gallery area of the lab/studio on Floyd, showing a number of historical cameras. It was fun and added credibility to our business.

Jim in Mathis Photo Museum 1991

Working just four days a week allowed us to do a lot of traveling. Louise and I love going new places and seeing new things. Naturally, one goal was to bring home beautiful photographs. We have been to England, France, Switzerland, Italy, Germany, Sweden, and

Norway - complete with pictures and stories in four-part harmony. We attended Fotokina – The World's Fair of Imaging in Cologne, Germany - and we were in Rochester, NY, the headquarters of Eastman Kodak, for the fiftieth anniversary of Kodachrome.

We were in London on Christmas Day, 1978. We were not aware of it, but our hotel was really a business hotel and all of the other guests had left for the holiday. We were the only guests in the hotel on Christmas Eve. So the hotel manager decided to close the restaurant and invited us to his apartment for Christmas. We had a delightful Christmas with his family and friends. We watched the Queen's address on the "tele," had a traditional British Christmas dinner, complete with Christmas pudding, drove around looking at the lights, and attended midnight services at their beautiful church.

Our experience in Rome, twelve years later, was a little different. We were victims of a pickpocket of about $300.00 before we even got to the hotel and were attacked by Gypsies twice before we escaped to Venice. We spent New Year's Eve 1990 in the Piazza San Marco (Saint Mark's Square), a beautiful experience that softened the encounters we had in Rome.

The Experience of a Lifetime

Wonderful vacations, a nice home, new cars, successful business, and a beautiful wife would seem like enough, but something was still missing. Louise and

I talked a lot about future plans and most of the time we were at a loss as to what to do next. We knew a lot of people who just tried to make more money and then tried equally hard to spend it, which seemed like a pretty worthless pursuit to us. We could, however, see ourselves getting caught up in this very thing.

One day JoAnn Capen, the wife of one of our customers, invited us to her church, Hillcrest Covenant Church, in Prairie Village, Kansas. We immediately felt at home. When George and Phyllis Chamblin visited us, we were quick to accept their invitation to attend a Bible discussion group.

Louise and I both had Christian backgrounds. She had attended a high school youth group and I had done everything I knew to do to find God. In the fourth grade, I attended the Assembly of God church in Coffeyville with a friend from school. When the Sunday School teacher asked anyone who wanted to be saved to raise their hand, I did. He prayed for me, but I have no idea what he said, and I don't remember my life being any different. Two years later, I went forward at a revival meeting at the Dearing Christian Church. I was baptized by immersion and was told that I had been born again. I felt a little different, but I can't tell for sure if I became a different person in any sense.

In college, I considered myself a Christian, and was even my fraternity's chaplain for a year, but I doubt whether my life was significantly different from any of the other men at college.

During our early married years, a couple of young men from the Mormon church visited us. As I studied with them, I soon realized that they were taking many passages out of context. Their doctrine just didn't make sense, but it did get me interested in reading the Bible.

By the time we got to the young married couples group at Hillcrest, I was hungry to hear what God had to say. As I began to study the Bible with this group of six couples, it really began to make sense. I learned that Jesus Christ had paid the penalty in full for my sins and that salvation was a free gift from God. All I had to do was put my faith and trust in Him. I let what I was learning change my life. I studied the Bible daily to guide me in my decisions and plans.

Louise and I together began to read the Bible and other Christian books, memorize scripture, and go to retreats and conferences as our schedule allowed. We both committed our lives to Jesus in the spring of 1978. Louise considers Palm Sunday, 1978 her spiritual birthday, but I couldn't be that precise. I don't even know if I became a Christian in the fourth grade, the sixth grade, or when I was twenty-nine.

I do know that over the next few years my life changed dramatically. We saw many of our friends come to Christ and we began meeting with others helping them become better disciples of Christ.

One life-changing experience was "Memorize the Word." This was a class where we learned three Bible verses a week for twenty-six weeks. Memorizing scriptures is probably the single most important discipline I have ever experienced.

I also got involved with the Christian Business Men's Committee. CBMC is an international organization with a long history of ministry to the business and professional community. At first, my involvement was just in attending the weekly prayer and Bible study groups. I eventually got involved with the men's retreats and in city leadership roles.

Children: To Have, or Not to Have?

If you would ask my parents what their greatest accomplishments were, they would probably say raising successful children. That idea has always made me uncomfortable. For one thing, it put a lot of pressure on us kids; we didn't want our parents to be failures as parents. But, also, just because everyone else was having children didn't seem like a good reason for us to have them.

Before Louise and I were married, we talked about having children. She didn't have any particular desire to have children, figuring that the parenting gene had passed her by. Oddly enough, I hadn't thought about it much at all. I had never thought about having children or what it would be like. After we were married, we decided to take a "wait and see" attitude. Most of our friends began having children, maybe because they wanted to, or maybe because they didn't know that not having children was an option or realistic choice.

After a few years we gave more serious thought to the question. We read a book called "The Baby Trap," by Ellen Peck which made a lot of sense. Ms. Peck gave arguments for and against having children and reminded her readers that having children was an important life choice. You didn't automatically have to have children just because everybody else is doing it. We decided that we would let other people bring the next generation into the world. Some of the arguments for children - who will take care of you when you are old?; they bring such joy; or how else are you going to have grandchildren? - seemed sort of weak.

After we became Christians, we rethought our decision because we didn't know any other Christians who had made that choice. It seemed that in Christian circles, emphasis on family surpassed the Biblical emphasis. For example: Jesus was not married and had no children, nor was Paul nor most of the other apostles. In fact, we know almost nothing about any of the families of any New Testament Christian leaders; it is just not mentioned. The Bible does mention Peter's mother-in-law, so he must have been married, but we don't know his wife's name or if they had children. We realized that if God wanted us to have children, He would certainly find a way. If not, then He had something different planned for us.

Because of this, we have lived in expectation that God was going to use us in a way that could bring honor to Him in spite of the fact that we did not give birth to babies. The freedom we have found to devote long hours to the needs of the coffeehouse and to individuals has been enhanced by having discretionary time normally devoted to children and grandchildren.

For example, one of the couples that we got to know was Bill and Kedra Manginelli. Bill was a professional photographer, a customer, and a good friend. Bill was an ex-Marine with a strong dependence on alcohol, still reeling from his Vietnam experiences. He was also a funny guy, the life of a party, and had a million friends. He and I could not have been more different in these respects.

As I got to know Bill, I invited him to a CBMC luncheon where a businessman shared how he came to know Christ. Through CBMC Bill also got to know Mike Anderson. Bill, Mike and I went to several of these outreach meetings together and Bill showed considerable interest in what the speakers said. I invited him to join me for a weekly Bible study. We met each Friday morning for about two years. Through his relationship with Mike and me, Bill made a commitment to follow Christ. We spent most of that time doing CBMC's Operation Timothy. Operation Timothy is a basic interactive course in the foundational truths of Christianity. The title comes from II Timothy 2:2 which says, "What you have seen and heard from me, entrust to faithful men who will be able to teach others also."

After we had finished the Timothy series, Bill said his wife, Kedra, was very interested in what we were studying and hoped there was a way for her to be involved. With that invitation, Louise and I began to meet with Bill and Kedra, as couples, every Tuesday night. We went through Operation Timothy again and then started studying individual books of the Bible verse by verse. We continued our weekly meetings until, seven years later, when Bill became an Elder at a large evangelical church in Kansas City. The hours we spent studying the Bible and its truths together, had well prepared him for Christian leadership. Even now we remain close friends.

During the time that we were meeting, Bill and Kedra had two young sons. Because Bill and Kedra had begun to allow Jesus to work in their lives, the boys grew up in a caring, growing, Christian home and are now adults involved in personal ministry themselves. This reminds me of the importance of taking a long view. It could be that the years we invested in the Manginellis were really for the benefit of their boys, or possibly for the benefit of somebody that they will minister to. I have heard it said that the most influential Christian of the twentieth century was not Billy Graham, but Billy Graham's Sunday School teacher!

Bill Manginelli is now a well-known leader and speaker in the Christian community and remains a good friend. Mike Anderson is an Associate Pastor at a large church in Olathe, Kansas. To many people I am best known as one of the two guys that led Bill Manginelli to Christ. Actually, I don't particularly like that phrase because Christ draws people to Himself. But I was there for the process. It was not always easy. One night while driving home from their house, I said, "This is either a total waste of time, or the most important thing we have ever done." After a few minutes I concluded, "This is the most important thing we have ever done." With that in mind, we decided that the single most important thing we could ever do with our lives was invest in people.

Over the years we have invested much time and energy in the lives of other people, but the Manginellis stand out as one couple where we saw the whole process through from the beginning and where we saw the most change over a long period of time. In a sense, you could say this has been our experience in having children – of the spiritual kind.

Jim, Louise, Bill, and Kedra

How to Best Invest Our Time and Careers?

Through much of the eighties and nineties, CBMC sponsored an annual couples retreat in Branson, Missouri. Louise and I served as the directors of this event and became more acquainted with the ministry on a regional and national level. It was here that we became friends with Charlie and Tammy Williams from St. Louis. Charlie at the time was the Area Director for CBMC. Charlie was a good friend and mentor, a voracious reader, he inspired me to read all I could about all kinds of subjects. Charlie began to tell me that he was praying that I would be called to become Metro Director for Kansas City. I responded to him that it was out of the question, since I had a successful business and had no intention of making a change. I know now, kowever, that effective prayer has a way of changing hearts and minds.

As time went by, Louise and I began to view Mathis Photo as a stepping stone to what might be next. We both began to feel that God was calling us to something greater and more important. In 1994, we decided to set a date of 1998 to close the business. That would give us a few years to make future plans, and make a smooth transition out of the business. Digital photography was on the horizon. We had seen the immediate conversion from Super-8 movies to home video and were quite sure that the same thing would happen to still photography in the very near future.

As we prayed about the possibilities, it seemed that God was pointing us to vocational ministry in CBMC. We went to St. Louis to visit with Charlie and Tammy. Charlie asked what it would take to get us to join the CBMC staff. I said that we were planning on closing our business in 1998, but if we were to sell it before then, that would be a clear indication. It was September 1995. We returned to Kansas City committed to pray about it.

Louise with Charlie and Tammy Williams

The very next day two men, who were occasional customers, walked into Mathis Photo and said they had come to buy our business. I reminded them that digital was coming, but they were persistent. I told them to come back a week later and I would have a proposal. They came back on the appointed day and accepted my proposal pretty much as written. The deal called for them to take over at the close of business at the end of the first quarter 1996. We walked out the door on March 31, 1996 with a cashier's check and didn't look back on the business we had given our entire adult lives to operating.

We were excited about our new life as vocational Christian workers. We took a few weeks off and then attended the annual CBMC staff conference at Glen Eyrie in Colorado Springs, Colorado. At the Glen, Ted

Hubbard, the staff consultant from London, England, gave us advice on a five-year plan. He said to do nothing but listen the first year. The second year, begin to process what we were hearing. The third year, begin to put together a plan. Take the fourth year to finalize the plan and implement the plan in the fifth year. Although we thought five years seemed like a long time, we chose to follow his counsel because we felt Ted Hubbard was one of the wisest men we had ever encountered.

As I began to meet with and listen to CBMC'ers around the city, a pattern began to appear. The average CBMC member had come to Christ in their twenties or before. The average age was now fifty-four. Everybody knew we needed to reach younger people, but nobody had a clue how to do it. This was also the case with CBMC nationally.

CBMC had been founded in Chicago in 1930, and the ministry in Kansas City began a few years later, just before World War II. After the war, Kansas City CBMC opened a Serviceman's Center to minister to military people and young men being drafted into the military. This operated from about 1950 until 1973, when the draft ended.

Homer Anderson was the main person in charge of the Serviceman's Center. In 1973, Homer proposed that CBMC conduct Mayor's Prayer Breakfasts throughout Kansas and Missouri. When I came on staff in 1996, CBMC was involved in twelve of these area Mayor's Prayer Breakfasts and about ten weekly Bible study groups. However, none of these activities seemed to have very much appeal to people under forty. We continued to ask questions and listen.

When I went into vocational ministry, my pastor, Dr. Garth Bolinder, told me that the secret of ministry is to lead a Godly life, only do it out loud so others can see what it looks like. That sounded like a good idea. Since I didn't have the luxury of a weekly pulpit, I began publishing a monthly newsletter. I have mailed the newsletter just about every month for almost ten years to about two thousand addresses. I presume that many of these four-page newsletters get read by more than one person. From the responses I get, this is one of the more significant things I have done with my life. I often receive phone calls from people telling me how something I said in my essay affected their life. I am occasionally quoted in the news media and e-mail versions have been sent to millions. CBMC International publishes a weekly e-mail called "Monday Manna," which often reprints my essays. It is translated into several languages and goes to many countries around the world.

Vern Mathis – 1970

My Father, the Auctioneer

About the time that we sold our business, my dad began to get very ill. I made weekly visits to spend time with my parents, relieving my mother so she could go to the store and run other errands. Each time I saw my dad,

I thought it would be the last, but he kept hanging on while growing weaker and weaker. My dad had always been very strong. I got some of his genes, so I have never had much trouble with being overweight or ill. I find that semi-regular workouts at the gym keep me in pretty good shape and it was the same with my dad; seeing him is such poor health was very difficult.

My dad had smoked for sixty years and his lungs were giving up. Sometimes people ask me if smoking is a sin and I say, "No, it is an IQ test." Actually, nicotine is an extremely addictive, deadly drug. I know because I saw what it did to my dad.

My father was in the Navy during World War II. He was discharged after being rescued at sea when his ship, The USS William D. Porter, was struck by a Japanese torpedo. He then married my mother and I was born in 1948. That makes me a classic Baby Boomer.

After a few jobs as a mechanic and selling cars, he decided to go to auction school to become an auctioneer. He was great at it. The LeRoy Van Dyke song, "The Auctioneer" is a pretty good biography of my dad. Some people even think it was written about him, but there is no evidence of that. In his avocation as a singer, it became his signature song. The line that goes, "He's the best hillbilly auctioneer," fit my dad as well as anybody.

When my dad died in 1997, the church was packed for the funeral. It was a glorious celebration. People told stories and we sang "Victory in Jesus." On my dad's grave stone is an engraving of an auctioneer's gavel, a guitar, and the musical notation to "Amazing Grace." That's pretty much the whole story of his life.

Determined Not to Have Any Regrets

As I looked at turning fifty it seemed like a good time for a mid-life re-evaluation. This is sometimes called a mid-life crisis, but that term sounds like it comes as a surprise. Actually everybody, on a regular basis, should ask themselves what they want to do with their life, and then get started doing it. If one is past fifty and there is something they always wanted to do, they should get started. Overall, I was happy with where my life had taken me.

One of my main regrets, however, was not continuing to play music. When I worked for Ben's Camera Exchange, one of my co-workers was a mandolin player named Sam Austin. Sam introduced me to the Bluegrass culture. I say "culture" because "religion" sounds like too strong a word. But in many ways, Bluegrass is a religion, its founder being Bill Monroe, and the main prophet, Earl Scruggs. I have had people tell me with a straight face, "If it ain't like Earl played it, I don't want to hear it."

My favorite bluegrass instrument became the Dobro. The Dobro was invented by the Dopyera Brothers in the 1920's, thus the name Dobro for Dopyera Brothers. The brothers were trying to make the guitar loud enough to be heard along with other band instruments such as trumpet, saxophone, or piano. This was before the days of electric amplification, so they invented a mechanical amplifier called a resonator. Today "Dobro" is a trade name owned by Gibson, but the word "dobro" is often used generically for any resonator-style guitar. There are specialty guitar builders who make high-end resonator guitars such as Beard and Scheerhorn, and there are low-priced Asian resonator guitars such as Regal and Johnson. It was at the National Dobro Picking Championship in Winfield, Kansas in 1976 that I bought my Dobro. It was made by the OMI company, which owned the Dobro name at the time, so I have a Dobro dobro. After allowing the Dobro to sit in the closet for twenty-years, I got it out one day and began learning some hymns. I committed to myself to practice on it at least an hour a day.

My other regret was not completing college. In 1998, I enrolled at Mid-America Nazarene University in a degree completion program. Part of the Bachelor of Arts program involved writing a research paper. I decided to write a paper with the title, "How can CBMC best minister to people born after 1964." People born after 1964 were under 35, the group commonly called Generation X. My research involved finding out who these people were and what they needed. This was a year-long project with lots of reading, writing, and talking to people. I determined that CBMC had been very good in the past at developing leaders. Perhaps God's foremost purpose for CBMC was to develop leaders. This emerging generation - Generation X - would become the leaders of the future, so this was the direction of my paper.

Addressing the Uniqueness of New Generations

I learned that this generation was all about relationships, more so than my generation, the Baby Boomers, and a whole lot more than my father's generation. His generation was described as being drained of emotion and the ability to build deep relationships by the Depression and World War II. My generation tried to overcome that, but the people under thirty-five were actually doing it. They seemed to really care about authenticity, truth, and strong relationships.

I also learned that just presenting the facts of Christianity was no longer enough to win the hearts of the Gen-X generation. They needed to see that God was real. They needed to see Him working before they would believe. Throughout most of its seventy-year history, CBMC had been an events-driven ministry. We have had Mayor's Prayer Breakfasts, seminars, retreats, study groups, prayer meetings, radio programs, books, videos, and everything else we could think of. But being a part of these former generations, we knew very little about relationships.

There was a time, not long ago, when all you had to do was convince somebody that Jesus was God and it would change their life. A booklet like "The Four Spiritual Laws" or "Steps to Peace With God" would be enough to cause a person to turn to Christ. Gen-Xer's need much more. They need to see God at work in the lives of other people before they are interested in considering how God can change or impact their lives.

Finally Answering the Challenge

When I became a Christian, the experience of playing in night clubs and bars was still fresh. I thought there should be some kind of place where people could go to hear live music, hang out with friends, and just have a good time without being subjected to cigarette smoke and noisy drunks. This idea of a Christian, or family-friendly, night club was always in the back of my mind.

So, when Gary Tenpenny challenged me on New Year's Eve 1999, I immediately responded, "We need a place. We need a place where people would want to be." I explained that I am no longer going to beg people to come to events. I just want a place where people can hang out with their friends and learn about Jesus. I had no idea what that place would look like, where it would be, or how it would work. But it was a start. I suddenly felt like I had the seed of a plan. According to Ted Hubbard's five-year plan, we were right on schedule, but it had been a very long three years and we were just now beginning to see the direction.

Six weeks later, a large and beautiful Starbucks opened two blocks from our house. As Louise and I were sitting there one evening enjoying our cappuccinos, I said, "This is it! CBMC needs a place just like this. We need our own coffeehouse; only we would have live music on the weekends, have Christian literature around and encourage Bible discussion groups. Starbucks could change the world if they wanted to; instead, all they want to do is sell coffee."

The next week we went to Santa Fe, New Mexico for a ski vacation. We spent the whole time writing down ideas on how we would operate a Christian coffeehouse. We talked about where it should be, who would work there, what kind of music we would have, artists that might show their work on the walls, and what colors we would use for the decor.

We were familiar with European-style coffeehouses we had seen in London, Paris, and Rome. There, patrons sip rich coffee from china cups and linger for hours. We were also familiar with the West Coast model which was more grab and gulp than sit and sip. The West Coast and Northwest-style coffeehouse would more likely serve coffee in paper cups and hurry you out the door. We decided to go for a mix of the two styles. We would offer sit down service with china for those who cared to stay, and paper cups for "to go" orders.

When we got home Louise and I started working on building support for the idea and trying to find a location. There was not a big ground swell of support among local CBMC members, though there was minor interest. Homer Anderson, one of our leaders for the past fifty years, saw the potential, but with his poor physical condition due to Parkinson's disease, he was not able to help much physically. I told the local board that they had three choices: (1) I could resign from CBMC and open a coffeehouse on my own as a sole proprietor; (2) I could start a whole new organization to operate a coffeehouse; or (3) Kansas City CBMC could open a coffeehouse and I would run it. They chose option three.

I did not try to gain the support of CBMC USA. Each city where a man or couple is on staff has a certain degree of autonomy to develop that city's ministry according to the culture and calling of that city. I knew, however, that CBMC USA had never begun a work quite like this, and felt that the quite radical idea would need to be proven in order to be understood and accepted. With that in mind, we incorporated as Kansas City CBMC, Inc, and applied for 501(c)3 IRS exemption. We considered the non-profit IRS status as our Certificate of Independence. We could proceed on our own if necessary. Since then, there has been a change in leadership of CBMC USA at the national level. I would be more comfortable proposing this type of initiative now, though no other CBMC city has opened a Christian coffeehouse to date.

Since I knew absolutely nothing about running a coffeehouse and my experience with coffee was limited to just drinking a lot of it, I decided to go to work for a coffeehouse to gain experience. I asked a member of our church and coffeehouse owner, Doug Brown, if I could work for him, without pay, with the idea that I wanted to learn the business. I worked for him at Toto's for about three or four months. There I learned about the equipment and suppliers. Next, Louise and I went to a coffee convention and trade show to see what else we could learn. I began reading books and all the trade journals I could find. I read a half dozen books about coffee and subscribed to three trade journals.

I spent months driving around town, visiting all the local coffeehouses, and trying to find a good location for a coffeehouse. I wasn't real certain about what I was looking for, but I knew a few things: we needed high traffic count, easy access, good visibility, and a place that was not too expensive. It took awhile, but I eventually saw the building at 80th and Metcalf. It had been Suzie's Fashions, a dress shop, for about forty years. It was now vacant and needed a lot of work. We signed a lease in January, 2001.

Another man who had worked for Doug, who also had a vision of coffeehouse ministry, was Zack Williamson. Zack had worked at several coffeehouses and a coffee roaster, and was currently a part-time youth pastor. We hired Zack to be the manager and began work renovating the building.

Homer Anderson

Homer Anderson: A Worthy Namesake

Before the coffeehouse opened, Homer Anderson lost his fight with Parkinson's disease. Homer had been very encouraging; his family asked that any memorial gifts be given to Kansas City CBMC for the purpose of opening a Christian coffeehouse. We received about $6,000 in memorial gifts in Homer's name - not enough to open a coffeehouse, but encouragement enough to keep going. The name, "Homer's Coffee House" seemed like an obvious choice. Once we started saying, "Homer's Coffee House" out loud, we started getting more excited. We knew this would be a place, had he lived a little longer, that he would have embraced and visited often.

Complications having to do with city approvals and our poor choice of architect and engineer led to delays. We finally obtained a building permit in July 2001. Meanwhile, we were paying rent on an empty building, paying Zack a salary, and running up debt. When the bids came in, they were three times higher than we were expecting. After a few hours of anguish, I threw away the plans, redrew them myself and went to work. If I had it to do over, I would trust my own instincts on design issues and only hire an architect to make the formal drawings. The experience I had working with Doug Brown and visiting dozens of coffeehouses proved invaluable, and I discovered that the new layout and drawings were a big improvement over the architect's lack of coffeehouse design understanding.

One of the less obvious secrets of Homer's is the lighting. Having a background in photography, I knew that nothing looks good under fluorescent lights. I am firmly convinced that fluorescent lighting killed Montgomery Ward. Everything in their stores looked ugly under those lights. They could not compete with the likes of Nordstroms or Dillards that knew how to effectively use halogen lights. I designed the lighting in Homer's from a photographer's point of view. Not everybody in every seat is perfectly lit. But most people look pretty good.

Once we got going, work proceeded quickly. We hired another architect to make formal drawings from our plans for city approval and were able to open on September 28, 2001. From the time we began making plans for a coffeehouse until we opened, we spent about $100,000. At first we took out a start-up loan from Valley View Bank. Larry McLenon, the President of Valley View, was a member of CBMC and had a vision for ministry. That and he knew us and trusted us. About $10,000 came from donations and eventually, after we sold our own house, Louise and I were able to loan Kansas City CBMC $90,000 and allow Homer's Coffee House to pay off all other debts.

Zack Williamson

Solving Finances By Recognizing Interests

Financial management has never been a big mystery to me. When I became a Christian I became very interested in the Biblical approach to money. The Bible talks more about money and possessions than any other subject; more of Jesus' teachings deal with money that any other single issue. I very much wanted to learn what Jesus had to say about finances and adjust my life accordingly. The Bible is clear that debt is a curse to be avoided. By the time I began to trust Christ, we were already pretty much debt-free, but getting out of debt became even more of a priority. We paid off our home mortgage in ten years and began saving money regularly. We were some of the very first people to open IRAs when they became available when I was 27 years old.

In 1995 we bought a new house for cash. We really liked our old house, but we were afraid that we would end up being there our entire lives, and we had seen the difficulties many people had leaving a house they had lived in for forty or more years. After a few years we realized that the new house was too big for our needs. We decided that the freedom of an apartment looked pretty appealing. We always loved the Country Club Plaza area of Kansas City so we decided to sell our house and rent a Plaza apartment.

Going from a large four-bedroom house to a small two-bedroom apartment was extremely difficult. It involved making major choices about what we wanted to do with our lives – particularly our hobbies.

When we came on staff with CBMC, we took a personality assessment test called the Birkman Method. There are a lot of these type tests available. All have some merit, but I believe they all should be taken with a grain of salt. Usually they tell you a bunch of stuff about yourself that you already know. One of the components of the Birkman is an interest inventory. It gives a long list of possible items of interest and then places you in a percentile of all others who had taken the test. For example: I was at 35 percentile for outdoor activity.

Louise was even lower. That explained why we never got around to using our camping gear. So we gave it all away.

The Birkman people explained that anything over 85 was no longer an interest, but became a “need.” To my surprise, I had three areas over 98. They were music, creativity, and literary. Literary includes both reading and writing. Since photography answers much of the creative part, I began paying more attention to music and writing. Being able to focus on a few specific areas of interest allowed us to greatly simplify our lives.

This realization made moving a little easier. We had to eliminate about 70% of our possessions to fit into the apartment. I decided that I wasn’t going to do any more woodworking, so I sold all my woodworking tools. I wasn’t going to work on cars, so I sold those tools, and so forth. By focusing on our core interests, we were able to vastly pare down the amount of “stuff” we were carrying through life. Since my three highest interests were music, creativity, and literature, I kept my camera, musical instruments, and books, and got rid of everything else that wasn’t essential for living. Louise made similar choices. We later moved to a slightly larger apartment, but the downsizing was a great exercise in personal evaluation and priorities.

Opening Day - September 28, 2001

Jim Mathis, Zack Williamson, Steve Gunn, Ali Brown, Kristen Lueck, and Sarah Newman

Homer's: The Dream Comes True

Homer's Coffee House opened on September 28, 2001. That weekend was Downtown Overland Park Days, so we participated in the parade - giving out free drink coupons. Our original team members were Zack Williamson and I as management, plus Ali Brown, Tim Deddens, Steve Gunn, Kristen Lueck, Bethany Munyon, Sarah Newman, Jason Bahr, and Joanna Gonzales. These were all high school or college students with no previous coffeehouse experience. The first few months were a learning experience for all of us, but everyone did great. As the kids would leave for college or other jobs I would begin to panic. How would we ever be able to replace such great people? But God is gracious and has always brought us just the right people at just the right time. Our staff is now a broader mix of ages. Since that day in September 2001, we have had a total of fifty-one employees.

In January 2002 we were awarded the Business of the Year Award by the Downtown Overland Park Partnership for doing the most to revitalize Downtown Overland Park. At the awards ceremony, Mayor Ed Eilert mentioned Homer Anderson, with comments about Homer starting the Overland Park Mayor's Prayer Breakfast. The Mayor expressed his pleasure that Homer's Coffee House was a fitting tribute to Homer Anderson.

Receiving Downtown Overland Park Business Award for 2001

An art gallery was part of the plan from the beginning. Roseann Copeland, a friend from church and a fabulous artist in her own right, volunteered to be our art director. Roseanne has faithfully interviewed artists and hung new art every four to six weeks. The quality and variety of the art displayed at Homer's has been amazing.

I Corinthians 13

Paraphrased for musicians by Jim Mathis

If I have the most gorgeous voice in the world, but have not love, I might as well be beating on a trash can. If have perfect pitch and know all there is to know about chords and harmonies and have mastered the last detail of music theory, but have not love, I am nothing. If I play in prisons, concert halls, churches, and arenas, but have not love, I gain nothing.

Love is patient to those less skilled. Love treats the audience with respect. Love does not need a Martin D-45 and a stack of Marshall amps. Love is not arrogant nor does it show false humility. Love does everything possible to please the audience. It doesn't get upset when it can't hear the monitors or if somebody is out of tune. Love does not brood over last night's gig. Love does not enjoy seeing somebody else bomb, but wants everyone to rock. Love takes care of other musicians and is always trying to improve.

If there is love, there are no failures. Great players lose their chops, great singers lose their voices, great songs are forgotten, but love will never die.

We will never get it right here on earth, but when we get to heaven, the whole set will be nailed.

When I was a child, I dinked around on my instrument, but when I became a man, I played with passion. Now I hear like a cheap speaker, in heaven, it will be 10,000 watts and crystal clear. Now I have to look for the chords, then they will all fall under my fingers and Jesus Christ will hear each note of worship played for Him.

And now three things remain; faith, hope, and love. But the greatest of these is love.

It's About The Music

The first weekend we had "Change Agent" play. Change Agent is a contemporary Christian band that I first heard at the Westport Coffee House during one of many "research" trips to the various coffeehouses in the area. We had originally planned to have soloists or duos at Homer's, but after I heard Change Agent, I redesigned the stage to accommodate a six-piece band.

We knew we wanted to have a great-sounding sound system, but after hearing Change Agent and other Christian bands, we decided to make a bigger commitment to the sound. I spent considerable time and energy on designing the sound system and working on the acoustics in the room. We bought the best JBL speakers, a Mackie mixer and Crown power amplifiers. We have a good selection of microphones and accessories. We believe that Homer's is one of the finest music venues in the country. For this reason, musicians love to play there. We have a long waiting list of performers wanting to play! I usually choose performing artists based on my instincts and the recommendations of others. We invite back those that do the best job of connecting with the audience.

I enjoy being around musicians. As a group, they are my favorite people. Since we have four hours of live music each week at Homer's, I have gotten to be good friends with a lot of area musicians, one of the greatest personal joys for me. I would never have gotten to know Bob Jenkins, Mick Byrd, Connie Whitlock, Dave Patmore, and dozens more had it not been for Homer's Coffee House.

Connie Whitlock is president of an organization called Kansas City Christian Music (www.kcchristianmusic.com). They operate a web site for Midwestern Christian musicians. KC Christian Music sponsors a songwriter's group at Homer's once a quarter. They also have an annual KCCM Awards show, presenting awards in various categories to area songwriters and performers. We have met a lot of wonderful people through this group.

I have always resisted putting music in categories. At Homer's we try to have a wide variety of music. The best groups have their own style and are not easily put in "boxes." As people mature musically, they tend to like an increasing variety of music. Musicians say a person who likes a wide variety of music has "big ears." Big ears is a good thing.

Musicians have a lot of other good words. Any musical instrument is an "axe." We go to the "woodshed" to practice. "Woodshedding" is a verb meaning to practice. With enough practice a person can develop "good chops." If you want respect from other musicians, you had better have some *chops*.

Another one of the early groups to play Homer's was "Electric Prairie." Electric Prairie is a family trio consisting of husband and wife, Paul Wenske and Nancy Meis, and their daughter Alexis Burdick, and a few others from time to time. Electric Prairie plays old-time Appalachian style music such as the Carter Family or Gillian Welsh. After their first night at Homer's, I told them if they ever needed a Dobro player, let me know. They did, and I played with them for about three years.

It was through Electric Prairie that I met Bob and Theresa Kaat-Wohlert. Bob, Theresa, and I wanted to play more variety, especially blues with electric instruments, drums, and electric bass. We formed a Christian blues band called "Sky Blue." Sky Blue now plays at Homer's once a month as well as other venues.

With Sky Blue I play bass, Dobro, pedal steel guitar, and sing. I have really enjoyed learning to play pedal steel guitar in the last few years, a life-long desire just now being realized. I started playing steel guitar when I was eight and played through high school and even on a few songs with the Playmates. But I had never played with pedals.

The steel guitar was invented in the 19th century in Hawaii. It is played by placing a "steel"on the strings to change the pitch and then playing various strings to make chords and melodies. In the 1950's people started adding pedals and knee levers to steel guitars. Theses pedals and levers raise or lower the pitch of strings either individually or in various combinations. The purpose is to make available a much greater variety of chords and voicings. It also makes a relatively straight-forward instrument into one of the most sophisticated and the most complicated contraptions anyone ever devised to get music out of. Of course, I love it.

After I completed work for my Bachelors Degree at Mid-America Nazarene University, I decided my next challenge would be the pedal steel guitar. Pedal steel guitars are all made to order by a handful of custom builders with waiting lists of one to two years being common. I was able to find a D-10 Emmons, just like I wanted, less than a year old near St.Louis. I paid a new price, but I could write a check and bring it home. My

Emmons pedal steel guitar has two necks with ten strings each; eight floor pedals and seven knee levers. I also have an expression pedal, a wah pedal, a digital effects processor, and a 300 watt Peavey Nashville 1000 amplifier. Now all I had to do was learn how to play it.

Then I discovered Jeff Newman. Jeff was widely regarded as the world's best pedal steel guitar teacher. In addition to his workshops, seminars, books, and training videos, Jeff taught private lessons at his home/studio near Nashville, Tennessee. I spent a week with Jeff in Nashville in 2000 and returned again the next year for another week. Before I could make a third trip hwever, he was tragically killed when his ultra-light aircraft crashed near his home. Jeff is a member of the Steel Guitar Hall of Fame.

Before one of my trips to Nashville, I explained to a friend: Some people play golf, others hunt or fish, or have a boat. I play music. If, as a golfer, you had the opportunity to play golf for a week with Arnold Palmer, wouldn't you take it? That was the way I felt about taking music lessons from Jeff Newman.

I learned not only a lot about music and the steel guitar from Jeff, but a little philosophy as well. Jeff said that talent is a term used by people who don't want to work to describe those that do. For example: "He is very talented, I wish I could play like that." Jeff's translation, "He sure works hard, I don't want to work that hard." Whether or not this is true, I think he had a good point.

Another desire I had was to sing. When I was young I was told that I couldn't sing. I probably couldn't, but because I was discouraged, I didn't even try. I did not sing in high school even though I was involved in school music and most of my friends were in choir. I didn't sing in the sixties rock bands I played with. We always had other lead singers and I was just a side man.

After I became a Christian, I would occasionally ask God why He didn't give me the ability to sing since I really wanted to sing. One day an astonishing thing happened. A lady turned around in church and told me that she always enjoyed sitting in front of me in church because I had such a great voice. I was sure that she had me confused with somebody else, but I thanked her any way. Later I recorded myself with a tape recorded and didn't see where it sounded all that bad. When I began playing with Electric Prairie, I asked if I could sing a few songs. They said sure, and I did fine – not great, but OK. They had no idea that I had never sung before. When Bob, Theresa, and I formed Sky Blue, I began singing about half a dozen songs a night. A lot of people now tell me they enjoy my singing.

The question is this: Did God give me a singing voice when I asked Him for it? Could I always sing and not know it? Or, as I expect, is singing a learned skill that just about anybody can develop?

The point is: I spent my whole life wishing I could sing and then, at the age of fifty-two, sang out loud for the first time. I have started a totally new business, began playing a very difficult musical instrument, began a singing career, and started a rock band, all at a time in life when I could have been heading for Florida or Arizona to take it easy in the sun. I haven't seen anything in the scriptures that says we should coast after a certain point in life. In fact, if we are "over-the-hill" it seems we should be picking up speed, not slowing down.

I have determined that if there is something a person has always wanted to do with their life – now is the time to get started. It is not being selfish; it is being obedient. God gives us desires and passions for a reason. He expects us to act on them. As John Eldredge said in his book, "Wild at Heart," "Don't try to figure out what God needs to have done, do what makes you come alive, because God needs people who have come alive."

A Unique, Eclectic Community

Homer's Coffee House has become even more than we expected. God called us to build a Christian community around a place that would influence the larger community and affect the culture.

Some of the first customers at Homer's were Mike and Connie Janouschek. Mike was a recovering alcoholic with a couple of year's sobriety and a fairly new Christian. Mike and Connie immediately made Homer's their home away from home. Before long, their daughter, Christy, was working for us. The three have been some of our biggest supporters. Christy has become the catalyst for building strong relationships between many young people. She has personally been instrumental in bringing people to faith in Christ through Homer's. Mike is constantly reaching out to those in need. He is particularly sensitive to those with alcohol or drug dependency. When Mike and Christy chose to be baptized in Shawnee Mission Lake, a large group from Homer's was there to celebrate with them.

Mike and Christy Janouschek being baptized in Shawnee Mission Lake

One of the featured Christian bands at Homer's is Second Mile. Dave Cedillo is a guitar player with the band. Louise and I got to be good friends with Dave and his wife, Jenny, when they were planning a trip to Paris.

Louise helped them learn some French and I gave them a few tips about the streets of Paris. Dave and I also started playing music together. We played a Fourth of July party under the name "Lo-Fi Radio." (Dave's idea.) But mainly we just got to be friends.

One day over lunch I asked Dave what he really wanted to do with his life. He said he wanted to be a cartoonist. I said, "A cartoonist? I've been looking for a cartoonist." With that Dave started drawing cartoons for our monthly newsletter. We also hired him to work full-time as a barista at the coffeehouse. "Barista" is the Italian word for "bartender," but is commonly used to refer to a person who makes specialty coffee drinks at a coffee bar. Dave has a heart for God and ministry, and quickly began building strong relationships with customers and the rest of the staff.

About a year after we opened, Zack Williamson left Homer's to become the full-time youth pastor at a multi-cultural church. By then, Louise was the Director of Women Ministries at Hillcrest Covenant Church. After serving in that role for four years, Louise left to help manage Homer's Coffee House. Louise and I both have the spiritual gift of hospitality. That means that making others feel comfortable and looking out for their needs comes easy for us. That gift, along with training in etiquette that we both received through the fraternity/sorority system during our college years, has helped us make our guests at Homer's feel comfortable.

Borrowing a technique from Southwest Airlines, we always hire for personality – train for skill. We can train people to make coffee, we don't know how to train them to be caring or nice. Or funny. A good sense of humor is a plus for anybody, and that is one of the things we look for in our staff. We believe that if we have a good time and care for each other, it will be attractive to everyone who comes through the door.

Every Homer's staff person has a funny story and a lot of them have to do with whipped cream. It is almost a right-of-passage to either accidentally spray somebody or get sprayed with whipped cream. Soon everyone develops a healthy respect for what a pint of whipping cream, pressurized by N_2O can do.

Before long, Louise and I realized that things had grown out of our control. People were getting together after work. Staff members were taking trips together. Large groups were meeting at Cedillo's house to watch movies or spend time talking. It was happening. What we had dreamed was finally coming true. We were becoming a community that people wanted to be a part of. People I had never seen before started coming up to me on the street and telling me how Homer's had saved their life. We have lost count of the stories and the lives that have been directly touched by the love of God demonstrated through Homer's Coffee House. When I am introduced to strangers as the director of Homer's Coffee House, they light up and say, "I love that place." That makes me feel great.

One day I asked Shandi Reeves, one of Homer's baristas, how many of her friends she had met through Homer's. She looked rather surprised and said, "I didn't have any friends before I came to Homer's." She met her future husband, Mike, her first day at work.

Mary Ann Bettis, a long-time friend of Louise, began working at Homer's and has been very instrumental in bringing people together and building relationships. Mary Ann and her husband, Mike, have a weekly dinner and Bible study in their home with about a dozen people they met through the coffeehouse. A number of these people are single or have no family members nearby and consider the Homer's community to be their family.

A young man came in one day with obvious physical and mental challenges. His name was Mat, and he soon became a regular fixture around the coffeehouse. Sometimes he could be disruptive and he often said inappropriate things. One day I was about to ask Mat to leave when a lady came in and called me aside. She said she was Mat's aunt. She told me about how Mat had sustained serious head injuries in a bicycle accident when he was eight years old. She also told me that Homer's was an answer to prayer, because his family had been praying that Mat would find a place where he could find friends and be accepted for who he is.

I assured her that Mat was among friends and that we would watch out for him. Mat began attending a Bible discussion group, soon began to trust Christ, and we saw his personality and attitude change dramatically. God has not chosen to heal Mat of his injuries, but He has used him in many ways just the same. God often chooses the disadvantaged to make Himself known.

One of my disappointments is that my dad did not live long enough to see Homer's Coffee House. He would have loved everything about it. He loved people, he loved music, and he loved coffee. After he died, my mother married Jarold Timmerman. Jarold visited Homer's often and loved the place, too. Jarold went to heaven in November 2003.

After Jarold died, my mother moved to Overland Park. The people at Homer's welcomed her with open arms and she now considers herself part of the Homer's community. She has developed a ministry there as well, reaching out to other people her age and in similar situations.

In the 1950's and early '60s, my dad hosted the "Dearing Hootenanny" in the Dearing, Kansas City Park each summer. It was sort of a "play what you brought - everybody join in - country music show." With that background in mind, we decided to have "Pickin' on the Patio" at Homer's. Pickin' on the Patio is an open-mike, acoustic jam session held every Monday night between Memorial Day and Labor Day. The purpose is to help build relationships between area musicians and to give people who might not have an opportunity to play in public a chance to do so. In 2005 we added a cook-out to the party, grilling burgers and bratwurst.

Pickin on the Patio – July 2005

Sociologist Ray Oldenburg, in his book, "The Great Good Place: Cafes, Coffee Shops, Bookstores, Bars, Hair Salons, and Other Hangouts at the Heart of a Community," talks about the concept of the "third place." Most people have two places – their home and their work. But a third place is needed. A place where they can meet their friends, where nothing is demanded of them, and where they can just be themselves, relax, and have fun. Oldenburg suggests that one of the problems with America is a lack of "third places." Homer's Coffee House serves this purpose of a third place for dozens of people. People from all age groups and occupations stop by just to see who is there. Usually they see a friend; if not, they make a new one. Unfortunately, there aren't enough places where this is possible. Even churches fail in this capacity. I don't know many people who stop by their church on the way home from work just to see who is there.

It is not at all unusual to stop by Homer's for a cup of coffee and see students studying, pastors preparing a sermon, business people discussing a deal, construction workers taking a break, or women knitting while watching their children play with Legos or color in coloring books. Free wireless internet access is an appeal for many, so we offer that as well.

One such person who stopped by and met new friends was Tony Maden. Tony had recently moved to Kansas from England. He had met his wife over the internet and moved to Kansas to marry her. A couple of men engaged Tony in a discussion of Christianity. Before long; Tony made a decision to follow Christ. Several of us began meeting with Tony for Bible study and discussions on a regular basis. I have never seen a person grow so fast spiritually as Tony. Soon his wife, Sue, came to Christ, too, as she saw the changes in Tony's life. Tony and Sue are now an integral part of the Homer's community and the larger Christian community in Kansas City.

One of our employees, Drew Ryan, had an amazing birthday: He went to different family's homes about every night for a week; he was given tickets to see a University of Kansas Basketball game, and people left special notes and surprises around for him to find. When I asked him how many of those people he had met through Homer's and how many he had known at his last birthday, he said that they were all people he had met at Homer's the past year. He had spent his previous birthday alone.

Even though the people make up the community and that is the main appeal, a few other things are necessary. The first draw is the coffee. After all, it says,

"Coffee" on the front of the building. The service has to be first rate, and the ambience has to be inviting. These are on going challenges and involve a lot of training and working together. (There's that idea of community again.)

Another purpose of Homer's Coffee House is to be a "demonstration" business. We know that we do not always do things perfectly, but we try to act as a living model for the proper way to run a small business in a Biblical way. Never making mistakes would not be realistic, but handling mistakes with grace is. A lot of the CBMC ministry is working with small business owners so having credibility and a reference to point to is very helpful. It is easier to say, "this is the way we treat our employees" than it is to say "this is how you *should* treat your employees."

Coffeehouses have a five hundred-year tradition. Coffee was first used by monks to help them stay awake while praying. Most of the drinks served at coffeehouses are traditional Italian drinks developed over the years at espresso bars in Italy and the rest of Europe. Some are American adaptations and others are signature or specialty drinks developed by local coffeehouses. Homer's has all of these types of drinks. We do the traditional drinks like espresso and cappuccinos, the American versions like lattes and mochas, and our own concoctions like our Caramello and the Funky Monkey. The Funky Monkey actually comes from my childhood. I liked to add chocolate syrup and a banana to vanilla ice cream and milk to make a chocolate/banana shake in the kitchen mixer. We use the same recipe at Homer's. The freedom to develop new drinks is part of the fun of working at an independent coffeehouse.

Like most coffeehouses, Homer's seems to attract a lot of creative types. We even seek out creative people for our staff. On our barista staff are actors, musicians, cartoonists, artists, writers, and other wonderful people. We love to hear our customers say, "Where do you find these great people?" The answer is two-fold: God provides each one of them and they find us. Homer's has earned a reputation as a great place to work. In the early months we tried to have a dress code, but we soon found that was impractical with the type of people we were looking for. Now we just make sure we aren't breaking any laws or food service codes.

We have no idea what the future of Homer's Coffee House is. We don't know if Homer's will continue after Louise and I are no longer involved, nor do we know if the community built around Homer's will continue after Homer's is gone. One of the motives for making Kansas City CBMC and Homer's Coffee House a non-profit organization was that it might continue long after we have left the scene. But only God knows His plans for Homer's. Meanwhile we will continue to listen for God's direction, work hard, make the best coffee possible, build relationships, and share the love of Christ in an authentic way. If your desire is to save the world one latte at a time, that is what you do.

Important Resources

CBMC USA, P.O. Box 8009, Chattanooga, TN 37414-0009, 800-566-CBMC (2262), www.cbmc.com (Operation Timothy and other resources for business and professional people.

Specialty Coffee Association of America, (562) 624-4100 EMAIL: coffee@scaa.org

Suggested Reading

To learn more about coffee:
Uncommon Grounds, The History of Coffee and How it Transformed Our World, by Mark Pendergrast., Basic Books, 1999

To learn about community building:
The Different Drum, by M.Scott Peck, Simon & Schuster, 1987

To learn more about third places:
The Great Good Place: Cafes, Coffee Shops, Bookstores, Bars, Hair Salons, and Other Hangouts at the Heart of a Community, by Ray Oldenburg, Marlowe and Co, 1999

To learn more about creative thinking:
Color Outside the Lines, A Revolutionary Approach to Creative Leadership, by Howard Hendricks, Word Publishing, 1998

To learn about operating a business by Biblical principles:
How to Succeed in Business Without Sacrificing Integrity, by Rick Boxx, Integrity Resource Center, 2003

To learn more about ministry to Generation-X:
Virtual Faith, The Irreverent Spiritual Quest of Generation X, by Tom Beaudoin, Jossey-Bass Publishers, 1998

To learn more about living:
Live It Up, How to Create a Life You Can Love, by Tom Sine, Herald Press, 1993

Index

Anderson ... 5, 7, 35, 36, 40, 48, 50, 51, 57
Bettis 68
Birkman..............54, 55
Bolinder....................41
CBMC USA.. 10, 48, 76
Cedillo 66, 68
Change Agent 60
chickens....................14
coffee 3, 6, 7, 10, 11, 23, 47, 48, 49, 50, 67, 69, 72, 74, 76
Copeland...................58
Denyes........................3
Dobro........... 44, 61, 62
Electric Prairie ... 61, 62, 64
Fender........... 13, 16, 21
Gibson 20, 21, 44
Hillcrest 31, 32, 67
Homer Anderson.........6
Janouschek..........65, 66
JBL.....................21, 60
Jeff Newman.............63
Kaat-Wohlert 62
Kansas City CBMC....2, 40, 48, 49, 51, 52, 74
Kansas State University 15
Louise 6, 14, 24, 25, 26, 27, 29, 30, 31, 32, 33, 35, 37, 38, 39, 47, 48, 49, 52, 55, 66, 67, 68, 74
Maden 72
Manginelli 35, 36
Mathis Photo...27, 38, 39
Mayor's Prayer Breakfasts.............. 6
Mid-America Nazarene University........45, 62
Mission Blues............ 9
photography ...6, 13, 23, 27, 28, 29, 38, 52, 55
Rodney Lay............. 17
Ryan......................... 72
Second Mile 66
Sky Blue.............62, 64
steel guitar.... 13, 17, 62, 63
Ted Hubbard 40
Toto's....................... 49
Vern Mathis, ... 12
Whitlock 60, 61
Williams.............38, 39
Williamson....50, 56, 67